questions and answers about

Ants

by MILLICENT E. SELSAM

Pictures by ARABELLE WHEATLEY

SCHOLASTIC BOOK SERVICES

NEW YORK • LONDON • RICHMOND HILL, ONTARIO

1st printing .... April 1967

Printed in the U.S.A.

For Billy Schilit
who helped collect ants

CONTENTS

Here is a picture of an ant.

The body of an ant has three parts. Find the three parts.

One is the head. Notice the feelers, or *antennae,* that stick out of the head. See the eyes.

The second part is called the *thorax.* The legs are attached to this part. Count the legs. There are six of them.

The third part of the ant is the abdomen.

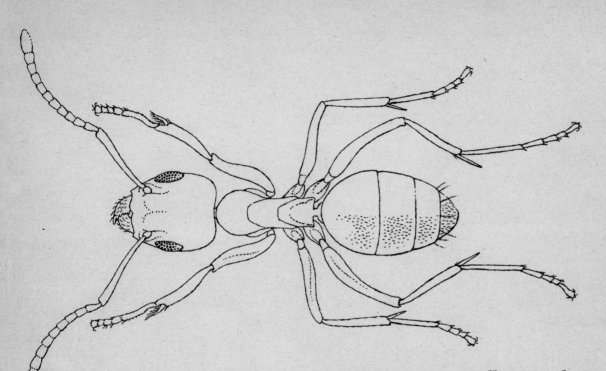

An ant is an insect. All insects have three body parts and six legs. Most insects have wings, but some do not.

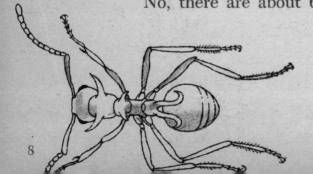

Do all ants look alike?

No, there are about 6,000 different kinds of ants.

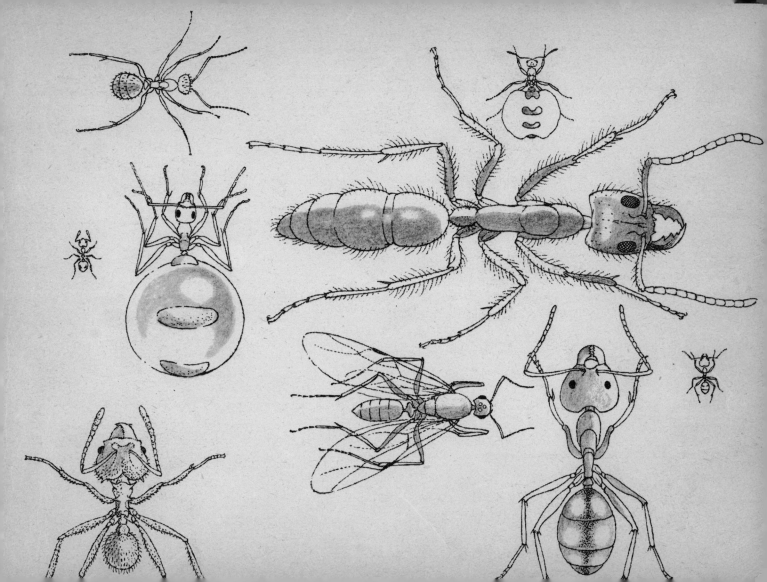

What kind of ant is this book about?

This book is about an ordinary kind of ant
I found near my house.

It is only this big ✺ but the pictures in
this book will make it look much bigger.

How do you watch ants?

First you have to find them.

Ants never live alone. They live with other ants. A bunch of ants living together is called a *colony*. The place where a colony of ants live is called the *nest*.

Where do you find ants?

This is how I found ants.

I walked out of my house near the beach. I saw some wooden boards lying on the sandy ground. I lifted up a board. Right under the board I saw a lot of ants. There were lots of little white things there, too. The ants picked up the white things and ran with them.

I scooped up the ants, the white things, and some sand with a large spoon. I put them all in a plastic bag.

You are likely to find ants any place where a board or a rock or a covering of leaves helps to keep the moisture in the ground.

What do ants eat?

Ants will eat almost anything as long as it is juicy. When they eat solid food, the food goes into a special place in the mouth, where the juice is squeezed out of it. The ant spits out the solid parts and swallows the juice.

Different ants eat different kinds of food.

Some ants collect the juice from flowers and stems.

Some ants eat seeds.

Some ants collect the sweet juice that oozes
out of plant lice.

Some ants eat dead insects.

Some ants kill other insects and eat them.

Some ants eat mushrooms that grow on
pieces of leaf brought into the nest.

*Does every ant in the colony have
to find its own food?*

No. The older ants of the colony find food
and take it to the other ants in the nest.

*How does an ant give food to
another ant?*

An ant has two stomachs. When it takes
food into its mouth, the food goes into the
first stomach.

This first stomach is called the *crop*. The
crop is really just a basket in which food is
carried home. When an ant has food in its
crop, it passes some of the food to the mouth
of the next hungry ant it meets.

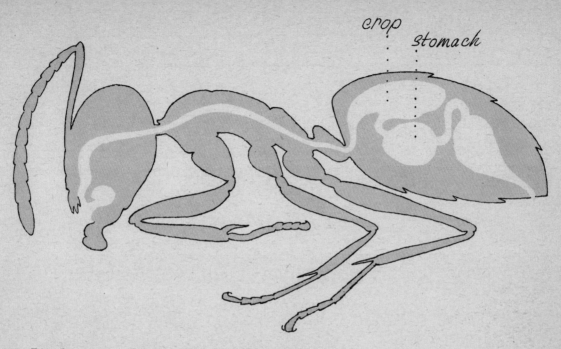

crop stomach

If the ant shares food with others,
does it get some for itself?

Yes. The second stomach is for its own
use. The ant pumps some of the food in its
crop into this second, private stomach.

One scientist did an experiment that showed how quickly food is passed from ant to ant. He colored some honey blue and fed it to six ants of a colony. They were light-colored ants. The next day every ant in the colony looked blue. You could see the blue honey through their thin skins.

Once I put a piece of peach on a window sill where I saw a few ants. As soon as they found the peach, the ants ran back to a hole in the window sill.

I did not know till then that I had an ant nest in the window sill.

Then I saw a lot of ants running out of the nest. The ants kept running back and forth from the peach to the nest. More and more ants kept coming from the nest.

In 10 minutes, there were 30 ants on the peach.

After 20 minutes, there were 50 ants on the peach.

In an hour, there were at least 100 ants on the peach.

They kept sucking at the peach until there was hardly any of it left.

*When one ant or a few ants find
some food, why do so many other
ants come running?*

The ant that finds food gets excited. On
the way back to the nest with the food, the
ant lays a trail of a special chemical. The
chemical comes out of a tube at the back
end of the ant's body.

How does the ant lay a trail?

The ant runs a short way. Then it stops and presses its body against the ground. It leaves a little spot of the special chemical.

Then it runs. Then it presses its body to the ground again and leaves another spot. The ant does this again and again. In this way it leaves a trail.

How do the other ants pick up the trail?

The excited ant runs back to the nest. The other ants smell the chemical. They rush out of the nest and follow the trail. They collect the food at the end of the trail.

Then they go back to the nest, leaving trails too.

The more trails there are, the stronger the smell gets. More and more ants come out of the nest. In this way many ants gather around the food.

food dish

nest

food dish

nest

Why do the ants stop coming when the food is gone?

The ants that get no food at the end of the trail do not lay the "food–trail" signal on the way back to the nest. The smell of the old trail goes away in a few minutes. So the ants stop coming.

What happens when ants with food in their crop go back to the nest?

They pass the food to the other ants in the nest that do not go out to collect food.

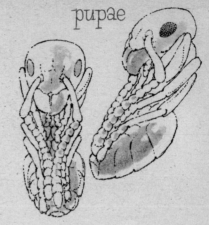

eggs larvae pupae

Do ants have baby ants?

The white things I picked up with the ants I found were ants-to-be. Every ant begins as an egg, becomes a *larva*, then a *pupa*, and then becomes an adult ant.

The smallest white things are the *eggs*.

The eggs hatch into *larvae* (**lar-vee**) that look like little fat white worms with a mouth at one end.

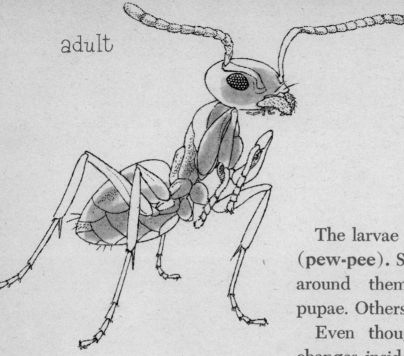

adult

The larvae grow. They change into *pupae* (**pew-pee**). Some larvae spin cocoons of silk around themselves before they become pupae. Others remain uncovered.

Even though a pupa cannot move, it changes inside its skin or cocoon. When the pupa is ready to hatch, the ants around it help it to come out by cutting open the cocoon or the skin around it. Now the ant begins its life as an adult.

27

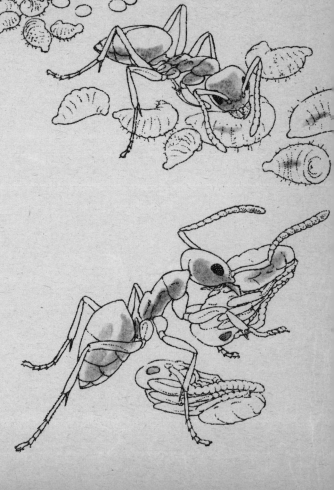

Do the eggs, larvae, and pupae
have to be taken care of?

Some of the adult ants in the colony take care of them. They lick the eggs, larvae, and pupae. This helps to keep them from getting moldy.

The adult ants also feed the larvae by putting food in their mouths.

Do the ants take care of the eggs
and young because they "love" them?

Adult ants take care of the eggs and larvae because there is a sweet liquid on them that the ants like.

Besides, an adult ant gets an extra treat when it feeds a larva. A sweet liquid comes out of the mouth of the larva.

When the larvae change into pupae, the ants go on taking care of them.

How long does it take to change from an egg to an adult?

It usually takes several months.

What does an ant look like when it first becomes an adult?

It looks like the other ants, but its color is lighter. It takes about ten days for its color to turn black like the other ants in the colony.

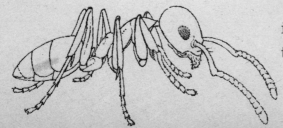

When a young ant becomes an adult,
how does it "know" what to do?

It is born able to do what other ants are doing, but at first it doesn't do these things very well.

Day by day the ant gets better at its work. This is because it gets older, and because it learns from the other ants.

What are other ants doing?
What is going on in the nest?

Some ants are digging tunnels.

Some ants are
cleaning the nest.

Some ants are looking for food.

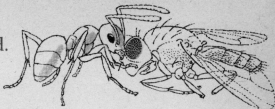

Some ants are cleaning themselves.

Some ants are just resting.

Which ants do what?

The younger ants usually take care of the eggs, larvae, and pupae. They also do building and cleaning work inside the nest.

The older ants usually go out of the nest to find food.

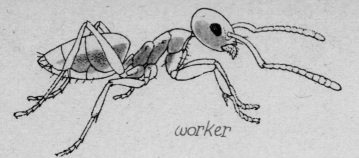

worker

Are all the ants in a colony the same?

Most of the ants in a colony are *workers.* These are the ants that take care of the eggs, build and clean the nest, and find the food. They do all the work of the colony. They are females, but they do not usually lay eggs.

In some colonies, there are female ants that are bigger than the workers. They are called *soldiers* because they help to defend the nest.

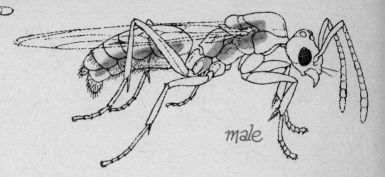

queen

male

There is a *queen*. The queen is bigger than the rest of the ants and has wings for part of her life. She is the "mother" of the colony because she lays all the eggs. Sometimes there are two or three or even more queens in very large colonies.

There are male ants called *drones*. They have wings too. But drones are much smaller than the queen.

At mating time, many pupae turn into drones. And some pupae turn into queens.

What is mating time?

Mating time is the time new colonies are formed.

On some warm day in spring or summer, toward evening, all the drones and queens come out of the nest. The workers come out too, and dash around and run in and out of the nest. Suddenly the queens fly into the air. The drones fly right after the queens.

The same thing happens in many nests nearby at the same time, and the air all at once is filled with flying ants.

These are not some new kind of ant. These are the queens and males of the ant colonies. The males mate with the queens in the air.

What happens to the males after this flight?

The males die.

What happens to the queens?

The queens fall to the ground. Their wings break off.

Each queen finds a new place away from the old colony and digs into the ground or crawls under a stone.

After some weeks, the queen lays her first eggs. She takes care of the eggs as they change into larvae and pupae.

Finally, the pupae change into adult ants. These new adult ants now take care of all the eggs the queen lays after that.

This is the way new ant colonies start.

How does the work of the colony get done?

Worker ants can do every job.

But some ants of the colony get more excited than others. These ants start all the jobs going. Then other ants join the work.

One night I watched one ant make about 20 trips back and forth. It was carrying grains of sand from one place to another.

The ant did not always go back to the same place to get sand. And it did not always put the sand it was carrying in the same place. It did not seem to be getting -any-where.

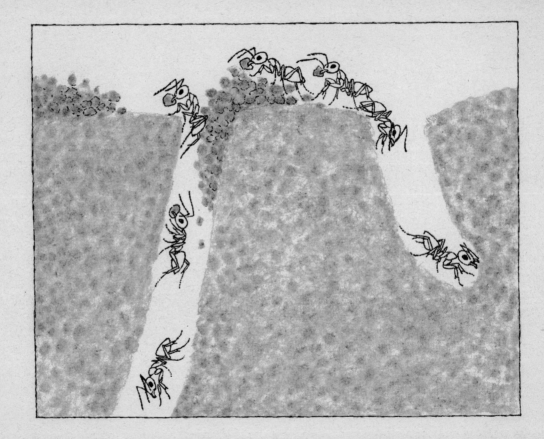

Ants may even work against each other. One group of ants may carry grains of sand into a tunnel while other ants are carrying sand out of the tunnel. Yet, after a time, the work of one group wins over the other, and the two groups begin to cooperate.

If you collect ants in a plastic bag and empty the bag into a new nest, you will see the ants run around wildly. But the next day the ants have already dug connecting tunnels through the sand in the nest.

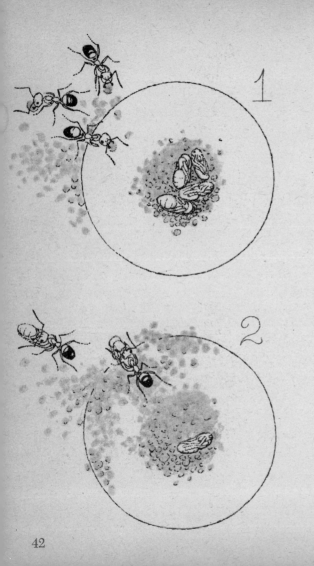

Do ants plan their work?

Some people say that when ants want to cross small pools of water, they decide that a bridge is needed and build it. Here is an experiment a scientist did to test this idea.

He made an island of sand in a little dish of water and put some pupae on the island. Then he put the dish near the ant nest. The ants threw sand in the water till they made a bridge to the island. Then they carried the pupae away.

You might think, "How wonderful! The ants saw their young and built a bridge to get to them."

But then the scientist put down another dish full of water with an island of sand in the middle. This time he did not put any pupae on the island.

The ants threw sand in the water again.

Ants usually move soil to where there is too much water. If they happen to use enough soil to walk on, then they have accidentally built a bridge.

One ant specialist thinks this is the way ants always act when their nests are flooded. They throw soil on the water.

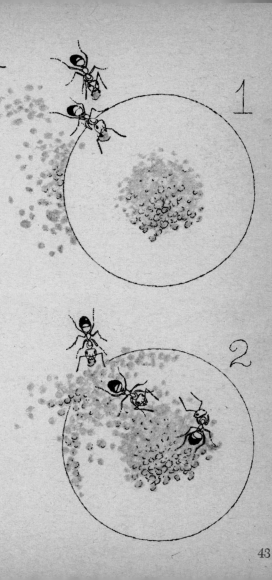

1

2

When you watch ants, you see that their antennae are always moving. Why is that?

The antennae have tiny organs of touch and smell on them. This makes it possible for an ant to find out the shape of something as well as its smell.

If you had hands that came out from the top of your head, and that could smell like your nose, you would have something like the antennae of ants.

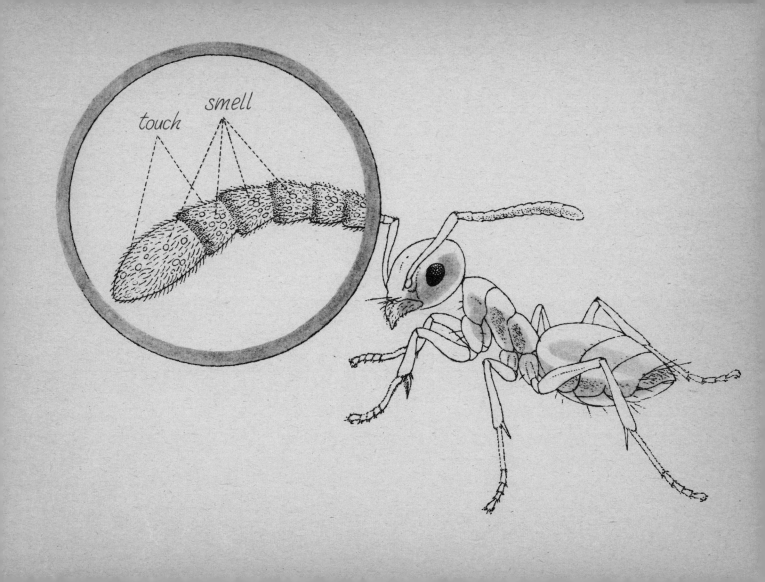

touch

smell

*How do the ants of a colony keep
in touch with each other?*

We already know several ways.

The adult ants are always stroking, cleaning, and licking the eggs, larvae, and pupae.

They pass food from mouth to mouth.

They clean each other's bodies.

They touch each other with their antennae.

They smell each other.

The chemicals one ant gives off can make another ant do something. (Remember the trail leading to the peach.)

When you lift up a board in spring
or summer and find a bunch of ants
taking care of their eggs and young,
what happens?

The ants pick up the eggs and young, and
run away. In a few minutes they are all gone.

What gives the alarm?

The latest idea is that the ants give off a special alarm chemical when they are disturbed. The smell of this chemical starts the other ants moving.

*Some people think that ants are busy
all the time. Is this true?*

Ants are no busier than other insects.
Each ant spends several hours during the
day resting or sleeping. It also takes a longer
rest at night.

When an ant works, it works hard.

How do ants sleep?

They huddle together in the tunnels inside
the nest. Each ant folds up its legs and
feelers and rests them against its body.

How do ants wake up?

They wake up the way we do. They stretch their legs and jaws. Then they clean themselves.

How do ants keep themselves clean?

If you look carefully at the front legs of an ant, you will see one place with long stiff hairs. These hairs are used like a brush. An ant lifts its leg up and pulls an antenna through the "brush."

An ant also licks clean every part of its body it can reach with its tongue. Any part the tongue can't reach, the ant cleans with its feet.

Ants also clean each other.

How do ants find their way?

Some ants can see well.

Some ants cannot see very well, and these find their way by smell.

Some ants find their way by both seeing and smelling.

Can ants learn?

They can.

Ants can learn to choose the right trail to food, even when there are six wrong ways to go.

Can ants remember things?

Many experiments have proved that ants remember the way out of the nest and the way back. Even after a winter of hiding in the ground, the older ants in the colony slowly come to remember the old trails.

Can ants figure things out?

Look at this picture. It shows what one scientist did.

There is food for the ants on a platform. Right below it is a heap of soil that almost reaches the platform.

The ants in the nest took the long way around for six months. If the ants had added a little soil to the heap, they could have reached the food by a short cut. But they never did this.

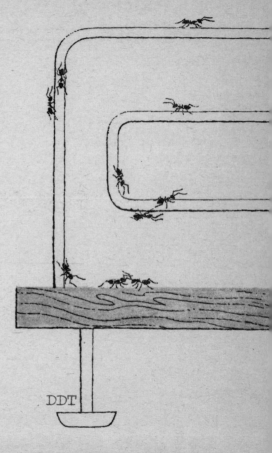

DDT

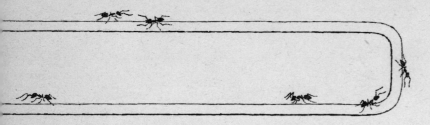
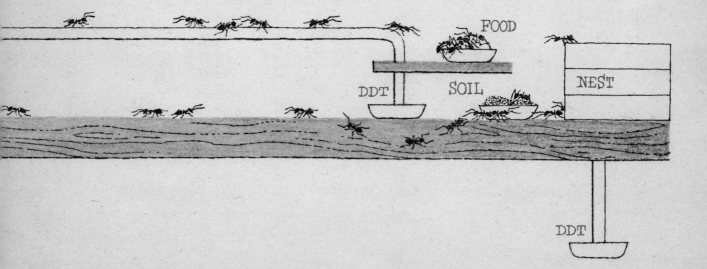

FOOD

DDT SOIL NEST

DDT

Adapted from diagram in *The Study of Ants* by
S. H. Skaife, Longmans Green & Co. Ltd., 1961

*How can we best explain the way
ants behave?*

Ants give off certain chemicals. And these chemicals make other ants act in special ways.

There is the food–trail chemical. There is the alarm chemical. There may be other chemicals we do not know about yet.

One chemical may cause ants to come together in groups in the nest. Another chemical may make them give each other food. Another chemical given off by the queen may be a signal to other ants that there is a queen in the nest.

Ants are always touching each other with their antennae and their legs, and these touch signals may play a big part in making ants do things together.

There is much more to find out. Perhaps we will soon know what makes ants work together as well as they do.

How to keep ants

You need a nest for them.

I used a clear plastic box I bought in the five-and-ten-cent store. It is not very deep, so there is not much place for the ants to hide.

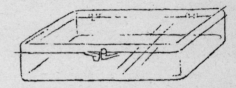

The box has a tight cover so that the ants cannot get out.

If you buy a ready-made ant nest, you will probably get something like this:

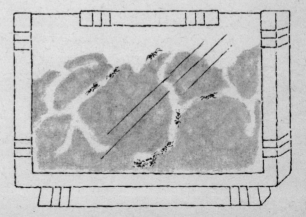

You can make a simple nest like the ready-made one by taping together two clear plastic lids of refrigerator dishes. Place the ants and soil on one plastic lid. Cover with the second lid. Then tape both lids together with adhesive tape.

The ants have to breathe.

I made two holes in the top of the plastic box with a heated ice pick. The heat melts the plastic. If you ever want to make a hole this way, get an older person to heat the ice pick for you and make the holes.

You have to plug the holes with cotton. The cotton lets air pass through, but keeps the ants from escaping.

You may have trouble with ants escaping from the nest because there are tiny holes you cannot see. If this happens, put your nest in a pan of water. Ants will not go into the water unless they are very excited.

Ants need water. You can add a few drops of water every day through one of the holes.

Ants need food. You can drop bits of food through the other hole. Try a drop of honey mixed with water. Try pancake syrup. Try jelly. Try fruit. Try a bit of hard-boiled egg. Try peanut butter.

I tried all of these foods, and they ate anything as long as the food was not completely dry.

Ants do not need much food. They are very tiny. One drop of honey can feed 50 ants. Feed the ants only once a week.

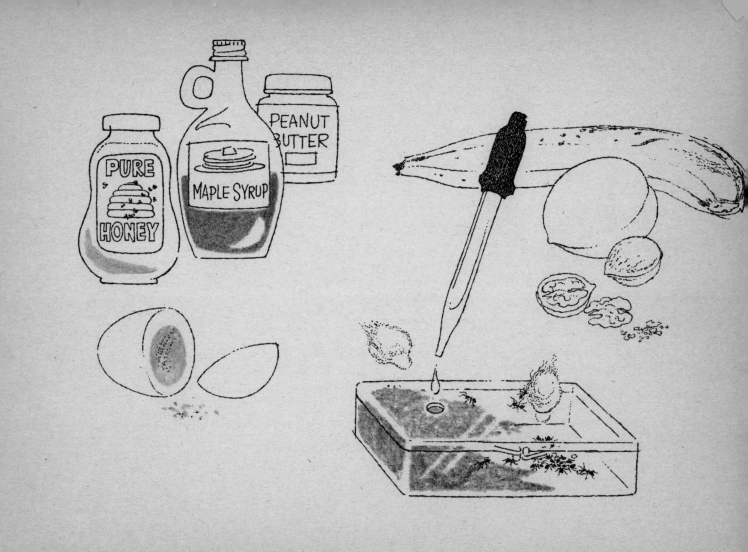

Ants are not easy to collect. When you uncover them under a board or a rock, they are alarmed and run around in great excitement.

Scoop the ants up with a large spoon or pancake turner and put them in a plastic bag as quickly as you can. Close the top of the bag by twisting it into a knot.

Then place the bag in a cold place. In cold weather, you can put the bag on a window sill. Or perhaps you may be allowed to use the refrigerator. In a few hours the ants "cool down," and it is easier to put them into a nest.

Cover the ant nest with a box when you are not watching the ants. This will keep them from digging deep into the soil to hide from the light.

Ants are fun to watch. You will have even more fun if you use a magnifying glass.

The ant species studied for this book is Tapinoma sessile Say

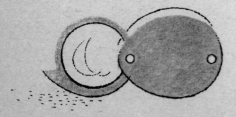